IMAGINE

Howard Hill

Copyright © 2020 Howard Hill
All rights reserved
First Edition

PAGE PUBLISHING, INC.
Conneaut Lake, PA

First originally published by Page Publishing 2020

ISBN 978-1-6624-0900-4 (pbk)
ISBN 978-1-6624-0902-8 (hc)
ISBN 978-1-6624-0901-1 (digital)

Printed in the United States of America

CHAPTER 1

It began twenty years ago; you know with the Chads down in Florida. That's when our two political parties seemed to divide into two separate camps.

Each one seemed to have its own separate and different ideology.

One went to the right, and one went to the left. And as you will see during the course of my story, there appears to be a very strong comparison to certain events of our past, for as you know, history sometimes repeats itself.

So my story will take you beyond the events of our present day and predict what could or may happen if our country should stay on its present course.

And Now Let Me Begin

When Andrew Jackson was President, he had to threaten South Carolina that he would send a fleet of warships into Charleston Harbor and blow the city to bits if they tried to secede from the Union.

While three years ago, our Democratic Party or at least some within it set off on a crusade to unseat a recently elected President, but with each endeavor, they failed but continued to push on relentlessly.

From the time of our declared independence from Great Britain up until the presidential elections of 1860, the issue of slavery arose with each and every election, but each time, a peaceful compromise would be reached between the north and south.

In a recent meeting between President Trump an the leader of Ukraine, certain words exchanged between the two men were seen by the democratic leadership as just cause to begin an investigation of our President.

The Past Is the Future

In the 1860 presidential election, Lincoln seemed to be the only candidate willing to speak about the evil of slavery while the other candidates preferred to avoid the subject.

His Cooper Union speech, "This country cannot continue to exist half slave and half free, for it will either became all of one or all the other."

As the democratic investigation of 2019 got underway, the democratic leaders brought forth their own witnesses but refused the Republican members of Congress the right to bring in theirs since the Democrats are at this time the majority in the House.

Days of very tense arguing and accusations hurled back and forth during the days of investigation, sometimes almost coming to blows.

Shortly before the Civil War, Massachusetts Senator Charles Sumner gives a speech in the Senate about the evil of slavery in the South when South Carolina Representative Preston Brooks rose from his seat and took his cane and began beating Senator Sumner on his head and body.

After days of contentious bickering back and forth, the Democratic leadership and majority in Congress took a vote and decided to impeach the President of the United States in 2019.

Now it must go to the Senate for trial and the House Leader must walk the articles of impeachment over to the Senate and hand them to the leader of the Senate, which is the law of our constitution.

But the leader of Congress refuses to do so for thirty-eight days.

Thus, the trail of the President and its possible impeachment doesn't begin until January 21, 2020.

CHAPTER 2

The Case Presented

On January 22, 2020, the Democratic managers began to present their case before the Senate.

After days of accusations against the President, the prosecution rested its case after a finale seven hours of statements on Friday, the twenty-fourth of January.

And beginning on Saturday, the twenty-fifth, the Republican defense team began its defense.

As old John Brown stands on the gallows platform in October 1859, he is asked if he would like to say a few last words. And looking out over a scene of US Marines and civilian spectators, he begins to speak.

He says, "There will be weeping and wailing in a million homes throw out the land, before the chains of slavery are finally broken!" With that, the gallows floor swings down, and John Brown drops to his death.

Justice John Roberts tells the senators to please stand for the Pledge of Allegiance.

Every senator, both Democrats and Republicans, rise from the seats. Place their right hand over their hearts and say the solemn oath.

During Washington's birthday, 1861, cadets in the chapel at WestPoint, are asked to rise and sing the national anthem.

As they rise to sing the Southern cadets leave their seats and walk out of the chapel as one.

At that time, most Southern states have left the Union.

One of the main accusations by the Democratic managers is the request for Javelin Missiles was held back by President Trump for Ukraine.

The Case Presented

When it came time for the Republican response, they said the Javelin missiles were, in fact, sent to Ukraine, and their request was met swiftly.

The Democrats countered previously by saying $18 million in aid was still being held up.

In January 1861, then President Buchanan ordered a relief expedition sent to Fort Sumter in Charleston, South Carolina. The mission was to bring only food and nonmilitary supplies to the fort, but when the supply ship attempted to enter the harbor, it was fired upon by artillery batteries within the harbor and forced to turn about and withdraw.

There are a few former cabinet members who appear to be traitors, willing to testify against the President with statements that may or may not be true. But either way, the President's conversations with foreign leaders should be strictly confidential if not secret. These former cabinet members say they listened in when the President spoke to the leader of Ukraine. "Is this treason?"

In the months leading up to Lincoln's inauguration in 1861, President Buchanan's secretary of war was sending cannons and rifles down South to the Southern states that seceded from the Union. Upon the President being told about this, he then asked the secretary of war to resign. Treason and traitors abounded.

Today, January 27, 2020, President Trump's defense team proceeds to defend the President vehemently against the Democratic manager's attacks upon President Trump. The call for witnesses by the Democrats is growing hotter, but the Republican senator in the Senate are just as much against it. Where will it end?

CHAPTER 3

The Impeachment Proceeds

In 2020, across our country and in all fifty states, militia units are meeting to discuss our national situation on how the Democrats are trying to impeach "their President."

Calls and messages are exchanged between militia commanders, not too let the traitors, as they call them, overthrow the President.

These militia members are uniformed. An armed with a variety of military weapons that all say they received from "people in high places."

They train in military tactics, and there are an estimated two million of them nationwide.

On the eve of the Civil War, there are militia regiments in every state, both North on South. The North believed that slavery was wrong, and the South believed it was part of their way of life.

These militia regiments appeared to be in two separate camps each with their own ideology.

As the Republican defense team is about to wrap up its defense of the President, the call for witnesses grows louder. But just as loud in the call not to have any, saying the evidence is in and a decision should be made "now" to let the government get back to running the country for the good of the people.

In 1861, before Lincoln takes office, President Buchanan meets with a group of Southern Commissioners to bring their states back into the Union and avoid the calamity of the Civil War. But their only answer is for the federal government to give up its remaining forts on their soil and in their harbor.

This meeting ends in failure as Civil War looms.

The Pot Simmers

On the university campuses, anarchist groups are trying to recruit students for possible violent protests if President Trump is found not guilty by the Senate. Many students shy away, but there are some who seem to like their brand of socialism. Even some professors encourage violent protests to topple the government if acquittal should happen.

By February 1861, officers and enlisted men who hail from the South are leaving their ranks and either resigning or defecting to their own home states by the thousands.

At the time of President Lincoln's inauguration, the army, which originally numbered only twelve thousand men, is now down to seven thousand men, and the navy has far less.

Our present-day Armed Forces is, of course, made up of Republican and Democratic soldiers, sailors, Air Force, Marine, and coast guard personnel, as well as our reserve forces and National Guard. One must wonder where they will stand if our presently divided country divides much further.

As Lincoln stands on the Capitol steps and takes the sacred oath of office, he then speaks to a greatly divided nation. Some would even say, two nations, but President Lincoln sees only one. He says, "We are not enemies but friends for you cannot have conflict without yourselves being the aggressor."

On this night of January 28, 2020, President Trump holds a massive rally in Wildwood, New Jersey, and 176, 000 people show up. Tomorrow, questions are asked at the impeachment Senate trial.

C H A P T E R 4

Lies and Deception

On January 29, 2020, the trail of the President's impeachment resumes with both the House managers and senators allowed to ask questions.

Democratic managers hand the chief justice notes of questions they want to ask the President's council. Then the lawyers get to respond.

As these questions and answers go back and forth, the division of our country grows deeper and deeper as the days go by.

On the first day of Lincoln's term in office, he is asked to make a decision in regards to resupplying Fort Sumter in Charleston Harbor, South Carolina. But the President decides to defer for the time being.

On March 6, 2019, Pelosi says, "Impeachment would divide the country should Senate take partisan measure to impeach the President."

President Trump himself states, "If the Democrats try to impeach me, our country will have a Civil War greater than the last one!"

Friday, March 31, 2020, the Senate voted on witnesses in the impeachment trial failed, and the leaders of the Democratic Party are up in arms as America now stand on the brink of the Civil War!

Saturday, February 1, 2020, Antifa, the group, occupies Time's Square in New York City. They carry and wave red flags bearing the hammer and sickle of communist Russia. They shout their cosmic slogans "Throw Bullhorns" and say they will someday topple our government and destroy our freedom and bring down the United States.

As Lincoln's inauguration draws near, South Carolina militia occupies Fort Moultrie in Charleston Harbor as President Buchanan hastens the withdrawal of all Northern military and civilian personnel from all federal forts, naval on all federal property in the South, but regular mail delivery continues, at least for the time being.

CHAPTER 5

The Apex

On Monday, February 3, 2020, the House managers and the President's council gave their final arguments in regard to the impeachment of the President of the United States.

Today puts into place the finale vote Wednesday, February 5, 2020's vote to acquit President Trump or to remove him from office.

As March 1861 gets close to April, the demand by the governor of South Carolina for the federal government to surrender Fort Sumter is growing to a fever pitch, and President Lincoln is receiving much pressure to resupply the fort or just give it up and prevent a Civil War. But Lincoln knows not to resupply the fort, and it would be paramount to surrender anyway, so he must soon make a decision before South Carolina acts on its own.

President Trump knows that the state of the Union must be given to the American people regardless of the climax of his impeachment. The date is set for Tuesday night, February 4, 2020. Will his address put at ease a very restive nation? Only Wednesday vote will truly tell. On Monday afternoon, Senator Manchin of West Virginia says he is yet undecided on how he will vote on whether he will acquit the President or not since he is Democratic, and the state he hails from is mostly Republican, West Virginia.

In the spring of 1861, as Virginia secedes from the Union, the northwestern part of the state refuses to go and vote to break away from the rest of Virginia and stay in the Union, thus becoming the state of West Virginia.

❧

CHAPTER 6

State of the Union

At 9:52 a.m., February 4, 2020, Senate Republican Speaker Mitchel McConnell speaks before the Senate in advance of the finale vote on Wednesday, February 5, 2020, at 4:00 p.m. to acquit or impeach President Donald Trump. His speech brings to mind three years of talk of impeachment by the Democratic Party through one accusation after another that in the end was false. Now each senator will get to speak his finale thoughts before the final vote is taken.

And on this night of February 4, the President will give his State of the Union address to the nation.

Antifa is also planning its violent protest should Trump be acquitted. One must ask themselves who is behind this terrorist group and what is their true goal—is it just one person or a "party" of people?

And while they are making their plans, militia groups across the country are also planning their own response to this group when the order is given. On Wednesday, February 5, the Democratic response was highlighted by House Speaker Pelosi, tearing up a copy of the President's speech after he finished giving his State of the Union address.

In the new Southern Confederacy, normal mail delivery is stopped, ending all mail service by the United States government.

Congressmen, as well as senators, are leaving the federal government and returning to their Southern states.

It is now April 1861, and as President Lincoln said in his inauguration speech, the national pot is beginning to boil over.

Today, February 5, 2020, at 4:00 p.m., the official vote is finally taken on whether to impeach President Trump or to acquit him. After the finale vote on both charges is reached, the President is acquitted of all charges against him.

The great strife is finally over, or is it?

CHAPTER 7

The Pot Boils Over

As this next chapter begins, what I write is purely fictional. It is left to you, the reader, and very possibly fate, to take us on the road of what may or may not happen after the impeachment and the days ahead become, after all, one can only imagine…

Could History Really Repeat Itself

It is early April 1861, and President Lincoln orders a relief expedition sent by ship to Fort Sumter. But as South Carolina and its governor get wind of it, a letter is sent by Governor Pickens of South Carolina to President Lincoln, telling him that any ship flying the flag of the United States that attempts to enter the harbor of Charleston will at once be fired upon at immediately. But Pickens, knowing it will be some days before the flotilla arrives, issues a finale surrender demand of Fort Surrender. He makes a deadline of April 12. And on that very day, as the US Naval expedition nears the harbor, at 4:30 a.m., the first shot is fired at Fort Sumter by South Carolina and the Confederacy. The Civil War begins.

February 9, 2020, the day is cold and cloudy, and on the steps of our US Capitol, a group of fifty schoolchildren, with their parents and teachers from the State of Alabama, sing the national anthem and "God Bless America." When up Pennsylvania Avenue marches a group of protester called Antifa. All dressed in black and wearing a black ski mask. They carry red flags, bearing the hammer and sickle of communism and shout anti-government slogans. As they reach the steps of the Capitol, they begin to hurl Molotov cocktails at the innocent children who are singing patriotic songs. Fifty of them are dressed in flames and die almost instantly. The rest are burned very severely. What have they done!

In cities across America, violent protests are staged by left-wing radicals. They return cars, loot stores, and attack anyone that they believe may be Republican.

The police across the country struggle to try to maintain order as best as they can, and for several days, the news media broadcast live coverage of police on protesters in the streets of our cities as America stands on the brink of insurrection.

And just as anti-Trump protesters fill the streets, those in support of our country on President do the same.

Police try desperately to keep them apart, but as more and more protesters and supporters take to the streets, so does the group Antifa.

Antifa violence intensifies as they begin to attack public buildings in our churches. But their destructive violence doesn't stop there. Police stations are also their targets.

The governors of the states under insurrection begin to call out National Guard troops to restore order, but Antifa attacks across the nation are too widespread for them to try to get a grip on, and the President knows if the nation's problem gets much worse, he will have to send in federal troops to restore order.

And just when things seem like they can't get much worse, certain Democratic leaders give praise to the violent action of anti-Trump protesters and ask those within the military and police who are loyal to the "party" to leave their post and join the "movement."

With that, some 25 percent of both follow their orders and begin to form a military within the movement. But even with this great defection, 75 percent swear allegiance to God, country and family, and their commander in chief.

But America's great division is not only seen by the American people experiencing it themselves but by our enemies as well…

CHAPTER 8

Get a Grip

On this day, the funeral for ten of the children is going on in Alabama. As the service is concluded, some of the fathers of these poor children gather and whisper to each other. These men are militia members. Their members are some 235 men, and their militia outfit has connections with other militia units all across the country.

But little do they realize that the top leaders of the largest militia units in the country have set a meeting to discuss the internal communist threat to our nation and what to do about it.

And it didn't take long for them to come up with a plan either. They will attack the group Antifa wherever they appear and even infiltrate them to find out their plans, who are their leaders, as well as who is funding them. They will strike as their headquarters if they have one and hit them at the places where they assemble to carry out their violent protest. The militia will also show up at a socialist protest. The militia will also show up at socialist protest rallies and be there to make sure that order is maintained and to back up the police.

So it didn't take long before Antifa found itself under attack almost everywhere that they show up, and socialist professors in colleges and universities across the country who espouse communist socialist theory to their students are bombed, and their buildings destroyed to prevent their doctrine from infecting more students than they already have. And as some two million militia members rise and unite and organize, the leftist do the same with the help of those who have defected from the military and police.

On this very day, the President holds a national security briefing and is told of all the treasonous acts by the Democratic Party and is asked to make a decision on how to stop it. He is shown on a large TV screen the violent acts of Antifa as well as the leftist protesters, and then he is told of how militia unite across the country have taken matters into their own hands. With all this, the President knows he must act soon, or else...

CHAPTER 9

The Call Is Given

In 1861, at the first Cabinet meeting, after Fort Sumter surrounded, President Lincoln is asked by his Cabinet members, "What will you do, sir? The country has been attacked, and our honor is at stake!" Lincoln sat back in his chair and reached into his coat pocket and pulled out a copy of the Constitution and then began to speak. He said he had been up last night looking through it for an answer to the problem, and that's when he said he found it. In a Constitution, there is a little know clause, it is called, the "Militia Act." "This act will allow me, the President and commander in chief, to call up our state militias. Therefore," he said, "I am going to ask for seventy-five thousand volunteers for the Army and twenty-five thousand men for the Navy to 'suppress the said rebellion.'"

In 2020, during his morning Cabinet meeting, the President is informed that militia attacks against

Antifa as well as leftist protesters are becoming more violent. Over a thousand of both have been killed as the Democratic leadership call for a calm while, at the same time, they give praise to anti-Trump protesters and demonstrators. President Trump tells his Cabinet members that he has come to a decision.

He says, "I've had enough of the treason of the Democratic leadership, so I think it's time to shut them down once and for all, so I will have them arrested and placed in federal prison for the duration of this insurrection. I must also get a grip on these militia groups too. So, therefore, I'm going to invoke the Militia Act, which will allow me to at least try to get them under control." So then the President directed his secretary of state to set up a meeting between him, the secretary of state, and the top leaders or leader of what they called themselves, the United Militia of America.

CHAPTER 10

Who Will Decide

The US Secretary of State told his top aides to locate and then set up a secret top-level meeting between him and the top leadership of UMA. And within a week's time, a meeting was planned to take place at a fine estate in Montana.

On the day of the secret meeting, UMA carried out two more attacks, one against a headquarters of Antifa, and the other against a group of about a thousand anti-Trump protesters. In the second incident, two dozen people were killed and wounded.

So as the US motorcade of five vehicles drove unto the property of the meeting place, they were first stopped and then directed by militia members dressed in their traditional camouflage uniforms and armed with M-16 rifles. An officer apparently in charge led them by a Humvee up the road to a large mansion-like house surrounded by a forest of trees.

The Secretary of State is greeted by what appears to be an honor guard of a battalion of militia. An officer standing on the bottom step snaps to attention, salutes, as the secretary of state exits the car. He is then escorted into the House and led to a large room. When the door opens, the view that greets him is a long table surrounded on both sides by what looks like high-ranking officers all dressed the same.

The secretary and his staff are led to their seats, and when they sit down, all the others standing at attention sit down as well. It is then that through another door, in walks who appears to be their leader. He introduces himself as General David, commander of the UMA, and then the meeting begins.

"I have been sent by the President to work out an agreement between the government," and the UMA says, "Secretary Powell."

The general responds by asking, "What type of agreement could you offer us that we might find acceptable?"

CHAPTER 11

Who Will Decide

In 1861, during the days that followed President Lincoln's call for volunteers, he met with Chief Justice Chaney about the issue of widespread treason in the North. And that's when he made one of the most controversial decisions of the Civil War. He declared that he was suspending the Writ of Habeas Corpus, between Washington and New York, and that anyone suspected of committing treason would be arrested and sent to federal prison for the duration of the war and held without trial. At first, the President's order caused consternation throughout the North, but after a short period, those loyal to the United States and the Union realized it was indeed necessary to save our republic.

On a cool March day in 2020, while the Congress was in session, the doors of the Capitol fly open, and in walk federal marshals with orders to arrest a number of them on high treason. Some struggle and some go willingly and for the time being, or at least till Congress can reestablish itself with the loyalty it once had to our country and people. Even the news media is warned not to put provocative news stories as they may find themselves shut down! Now the message is clear: return to patriotic loyalty or leave the country. The time has come to say and show which side you stand on, whether you want to or not. As of April 1, 2020, the country is under martial law by order of the President. Those on the right side with the right, and those with the left side with the left. At sea on this day, two US warships, one under the command of a Republican captain and the other under the command of a Democratic captain, exchange shots across each other's bow. Is this the beginning of a second American Civil War?

CHAPTER 12

Cross Swords

In July 1861, after almost four months of inaction, President Lincoln gives the order for the Grand Army of the Republic to march upon Richmond, bur army intelligence tells him that before the army can take the Rebel Capital, it will have to defeat a sizable enemy force along a creek called Bull Run.

In summer of 2020, along a creek out in Michigan, ten thousand troops, loyal to the Democratic Party and the leftist demonstrations, are encamped to protect a planned demonstration latter that day when eight thousand militia members in a nearby border state get wind of it and move swiftly to intercede against it. And as the militia arrives at the site of the demonstration, they are fired upon by protesters in the crowd, and several militias are killed Democratic Party troops hearing this incident move swiftly to assist the demonstrators, but upon arrival at the scene, they are fired upon by militia members as revenge for the recent killing of some fifteen members by the protesters.

The first battle between the left and the right erupts as protesters scatter to take cover. Blocks of buildings are destroyed or ruined, and for the second time in American history, Americans kill fellow Americans in battle. Some five thousand dead from both sides lies dead because of the great split in the United States. The government feels powerless to stop it. Can peace reign again?

CHAPTER 13

The Meeting

The secretary of state answers General David's questions with a stern look on his face. To start, he says, "The President would like to place the UMA under the control of the federal government."

With that, the general sits up straight in his chair and appears to be shocked at what was just said.

Then the secretary tried to explain just what he meant. "What I mean to say is you will have the backing and support of the federal government when it comes to any judicial repercussion that may arise from your actions." Then after a pause, he says, "That is if the UMA stays within the guideline set forth by the President."

Then General David, looking around the room at his commanders, ask the secretary of state, "So what are these guidelines?"

Responding once to the questions asked of him, he explains to the general of the UMA. "Well, for one thing, the killing of unarmed protesters is unexpectable, but your attacks against Antifa is. And in regards to the recent armed conflict in Michigan, there will soon be a strong response by the federal government against those of the People's Army. If you accept his agreement," the secretary said, "we will supply the UMA with arms and supplies that you may require to carry out your mission."

General David once again looked around the room at his militia commanders and get their nod of approval and said he would accept the government's offer.

And with that said, this new strange alliance was formed. The President this day orders on-air attack upon forces of the DPA, or Democratic People's Army, as the Democratic Party demands the release of all its leaders recently imprisoned.

And the Pentagon reports a sizable fleet of Russian warships approaching the East Coast of the United States.

CHAPTER 14

From Enemy to Ally

During February 1862, a US warship called the *San Jacinto*, fires a warning shot across the bow of the British Merchant Steamer Trent. The US ship sends a boarding party to board the Trent in search of a most strange cargo. While on board, they discover two Confederate Commissioners. They are on their way to England to meet with Queen Victoria to present to her a document requesting British intervention in the American Civil War on behalf of the Confederacy.

On this night in 2020, the Democratic hopefuls for the presidency hold a debate. This seems so odd since the nation appears to have slipped into another Civil War. But what is seen by the average American is that the party is split, and all want peace and healing. Each candidate appeals to the President to release their imprisoned party leaders. But at this time, he will have none of it, not at least until he can put an end to the growing insurrection spreading across our land.

Later on the same night, the secretary of state receives an urgent message from the Russian Foreign Minister asking for a 3:00 a.m. meeting in Washington. The secretary presents the request to the President to approve the meeting.

At 2:00 a.m., a Russian government plane touches down at Andrews Joint Air Force Base, and a dark motorcade heads for the State Department. And at 3:00 a.m., the two top government leaders sit down for a top-secret talk.

"My President, Mr. Secretary will not allow any intervention by any outside nation into your internal conflict. And our fleet that you well know is approaching your coast is not an enemy but an ally. With the permission of the United States, it will remain off your coast until you feel your situation is well in hand or secure."

CHAPTER 15

Strange Bed Fellows

Two years into the Civil War, in 1864, President Lincoln gives permission for the Great White Russian fleet to dock in New York Harbor. It will remain there for the next year as a deterrent against British intervention. It was during this year that Secretary Seward works out a deal with Russia to sell the United States Alaska.

As the election of 2020 heats up, so does our Civil War with battles between elements of America's Armed Forces, battling each other along party lines. And the UMA has virtually destroyed Antifa, or maybe it is because its members are too fearful to show themselves in the open. But just when things seem to have settled down a bit, a series of bombs exploded across our land. And when some of the culprits are captured by the police, they admit they do so for the DPA. At sea, a US submarine commanded by a captain who is sympathetic to the DPA fires a torpedo at the US-guided missile Fraguart and strikes its target, sinking the ship but not before debt charges are launched after the torpedo was detected and blows the submarine to bits as the warship sinks into the sea killing most of its crew. By now, the President and those loyal to him at the Pentagon realize if they don't crush this defection by a quarter of the Armed Forces soon, it may spread to our overseas bases and possibly even to our nuclear forces.

And on this day, upon request by the Russian government, the President agrees to let the Russian fleet stationed off the East Coast of the United States to anchor and dock at Norfolk Naval Base for the time being. Our government and military leaders hope this is not a Trojan horse. Even our allies cast a wary eye at this potential new military alliance. Could this be an era of new peace between the United States and Russia or a prelude to a Third World War?

CHAPTER 16

Neutral as Can Be

After the first big battle of our first Civil War, the average citizen, both North and South, found themselves caught in the middle of a conflict that none of them really wanted. Though the Southern people would eventually find the war on their doorsteps, the Northern people, unless they lived in Sharpsburg or Gettysburg, read about the war on bulletin boards or newspapers or letters. But the division between them was deep and dangerous as the South had slavery and was seen by the North as the great slave power. The North, on the other hand, did believe in freedom for all.

In the 2020 election year, the average person pretty much didn't care about the petty politics and bickering between them as far as parties are concerned. And they watch nervously daily and nightly on their TV screens the scenes of death and strife and outright Civil War. And as they go about their daily routines, they can hear explosions in the distance and thank God that it wasn't them this time. But as a whole, the country is as badly divided now as it was back in 1860. Only this time, it is along party lines with one party, embarrassing capitalism, while the other, or at least a large part of it, embarrassing socialism. Much of the Democratic people don't even know why their party has moved so far to the left.

Because after all, liberalism is one thing, but socialism is quite another. So it might be up to the people themselves to come together once and for all and put an end to this madness.

As the protest and demonstrations grow larger and larger, with both sides filling city streets with tens of thousands of people, representing both right and left, America's allies and enemies grow more worried with each passing day of the Civil War and national strife.

CHAPTER 17

Repercussion

All Civil Wars have an adverse effect on a nation's economy, and ours was no exception. With fighting going on between elements of America's Armed Forces, as well as street battles being fought between militia units and Antifa, and clashes between pro-Trump and anti-Trump protesters, the American economy came to a stagnant halt, as even the stock market began to fall.

Fearing this could ruin his chance of reelection, the President orders his joint chiefs to, once and for all, crush the DPA army with brutal force and also assist the AMA to put an end to all the anti-government protest in the streets too.

When those forces come together and the government attacks begin to draw world condonation, the democratic candidate for the presidency has a field day with their combined criticism of the

President and his domestic policy. But he doesn't care what they hurl at him since a part of their party he has declared treasonous anyway. And once again, he offers those he had arrested and imprisoned a chance at release—that is if they all take an oath of allegiance to our flag and country and do so on national television. Of course, he states that they must all do this collectively for their complete release from federal prison for if one or any refuse, they, as a group, will remain in failing.

Oddly enough, 50 percent of the American public supports this order. And two-thirds of the rest are borderline with many within the DPA army beginning now to have second thoughts about where they stand.

But just as some sanity came to be seen in the distance, a most-disturbing message arrives at the Pentagon.

A colonel in charge of a nuclear missile silo is threatening to destroy an American city with a thirty-megaton nuclear weapon…

CHAPTER 18

The Unlongineable

After having received this shocking report, the President asks his commanders what can possibly be done to prevent this possible renegade officer from carrying out his threat. And in awed silence, only one of them speaks.

"Sir, if he should fire his missile, there is a fifty-fifty chance he will succeed. If the media gets wind of this, imagine the panic that will spread across our country. And what will our enemies do too?"

"I want this prevented without them getting wind of it. Do I make myself crystal clear?"

"Yes, sir," they all respond as one.

And later on this same day, the British ambassador to the United States tells our secretary of state that Britain cannot stand with the United States that is if Russia is serving a potential split between the world's two greatest allies. The secretary of state tries desperately to reassure the British ambassador that Russia's offer to help the United States could actually be beneficial not only to the United States but to Britain and NATO as a whole.

At midnight of the following day, the President, while in a late-night Cabinet meeting about that nuclear missile base commander, an aide to the President walks into the room and hands the President a letter. He takes and reads it and looks quizzical at the men gathered around the room. He then tells them that it was shot down by one of our antiballistic missiles. He then states he is not sure what or where its destination was, but thank God, they destroyed it in time! Just as the whole room takes a deep breath of relief, the aide brings him a second message, which is handed to the President. A second missile was fired fifteen minutes ago and was en route to North Korea when it too was shot down by one of their interceptor missiles. This time launched by one of their warships in the Pacific.

The President asks, "What does this missile base commander want? Will he try again?"

CHAPTER 19

All Together Now

By the following morning, no further missiles were fired because the airmen within. the love, knowing what was happening, had arrested the base commanders, as well as those with him, and put an end to this mutiny themselves. But not before a Cabinet member leaks to CNN the story. Soon, news of this horrific incident is being announced by all the news stations. Both pro- and anti-government protest groups are befuddled, and the American people who refuse to take sides in this political Civil War, now seem to have had enough of this madness. So a group that calls themselves "People for Peace" announces they will hold a rally in Washington on July 25 in front of the Washington Memorial, and as word of it goes out across our land, interest begins to grow. And as people all across America start to travel to the nation's capital, they drive or fly by areas where brutal and bloody fighting has taken place between elements of our military or between the AMA and Antifa. The average person has seen on their TVs, computers, or phones the grisly pictures of America's Civil War or has seen columns of troops and tanks move along their streets or avenues, but they, at least most, have not seen for themselves the carnage that Civil War causes.

They are, as they pass by, shocked and dismayed at what has happened to the country they love and vowed they will put an end to this senseless calamity once and for all or die trying.

On that sunny day in July that the protest was to take place what was thought to bring only a few thousand interested supporters, it instead drew over a million people of all factions and all faces an race, all there for one reason—to bring peace and harmony back to our country and unite us all once again.

After a day of speeches at the mall, the marchers turned and headed for the capitol building where they pleaded in concert for both sides to stop fighting on come back as one nation and people…

✤

CHAPTER 20

When Peace Prevails

Sitting in their federal prison, the Democratic leaders sent there by Trump for treason realize it was their initial call for the insurrection that has put America into its present state of despair and also knowing it also has caused many within their party to turn their backs on them. They collectively tell the warden of the prison there in which they respectfully would like to send a message would entail, and they all smile and say as one, an agreement!

And when President Trump receives their message, he reads and smiles and says to his aides, "Well, I see they have finally come to their good senses."

At noon on the first of August 2020, fifty Democrats stand side by side and take the Oath of Allegiance before a televised audience nationwide, and afterward, one by one, sign their loyalty oath paper and then their resignation paper. With that, they are released from federal prison and forever are banned from holding any type of public office. And as a final demand by the President for their release, he tells them they must make a joint statement to all those on the left to end this Civil War.

And at 1:00 p.m., former Representative Nadler stands at a prison podium with an American flag stretched across a wall above and behind him and flanked by his compatriots. He begins to speak to the nation as what he is about to say is being televised.

"To the men and women of the resistance and the Democratic People's Army, I say it is now time to end our civil strife and return to the business of just being good Americans for a call of mine is to the left as well as the right. From this point on, peace, true peace, should be our one and only desire. And to those within our Armed Forces, return to your units, and those in the resistance, go be with your families."

CHAPTER 21

For the Love of Country

When word of call of the Democratic leadership for basically a surrender of them and their cause reached the commanders of the Democratic People's Army, as well as the leaders of the movement, there was great consternation throughout their sagging ranks. And with no apparent support from the average American, even middle American, what then was their reason to keep up the struggle that caused a Civil War and a division among our people as great as the last one? They wondered.

With many having left their homes and families and have given up so much and for what now they all wondered, their leaders sent out fliers for peace of some kind even though many within the ranks of the DPA felt disgrace by even the mere thought of it because, after all, these people were Americans and not a foreign enemy.

And as word of talk of peace hits the media and the open airwave, the American public rejoices as the stock market rebounds. Even the Democratic Party, though as split as it was, makes a strong attempt to come back together for the good of the country, as well as for those of their party running for the presidency.

So the first thing that happens is a call for an end of armed conflict between the two sides and an end to protest in the streets. But how will the American Militia Army deal with this new agreement? Will they fall in line with the rest, or will they splinter off into their own direction? That remains to yet be seen, doesn't it?

On August 1, the President makes a televised announcement to the American people and to the world as well. Everyone everywhere seems to be watching and listening to see and hear what the President of the United States will say…

CHAPTER 22

When Two Hearts Are One

At 9:00 p.m., the doors open, and the President walks to the podium, looks into the camera, and begins to speak the nation:

> My fellow Americans, I'm pleased to announce to you tonight that a tentative peace agreement has been worked out and agreed upon by the United States and the Democratic People's Army. With great thanks to patriotic leaders like Nadler, Pelosi, and Schumer, America tomorrow will awake to a new bright morning of peace and, of course, prosperity. But I must also give equal praise to those of my party who stood

valiantly with our country and people of both parties in a most _______ gesture that any government on the face of the earth has done on the face of Civil War as well as great civil strife because we must all never forget. And that is that we are all Americans and all with the same hopes and dreams for our children and ourselves.

And also tonight, I am going to ___ my previous order, banning those of our government arrested for treason from serving in public office. They sense they all have freely taken a loyalty oath and may return to their government post if they wish to.

So finally, my fellow Americans, may peace and harmony be with us.

Good night, and may God bless America, again…

On August 5, the leaders of the Republican and Democratic Party sit in the Capitol building in Washington and sign the final agreement, thus officially ending America's Second Civil War.

On April 9, 1865, Generals Grant and Lee sit down and work out the finale surrender of the

Confederate Army of Northern Virginia and the Army of the Potomac, thus ends America's First Civil War.

51

The End

Epilogue

As you have just read, we can all avoid the calamity in my book if we are only willing to listen, consider, understand, and compromise.

Because if we don't, what other choice do we as Americans have? Our national course is clear, whether we come together again as we once were and live up to the values of our Founding Fathers, or we face the downfall of our beloved country or, at the very least, as we once knew it for America doesn't want to end up as Rome did, that is destroyed from within.

That is why we have elections, and that is why we are still, and will remain, the last great hope on earth.

"With a deep love for all my fellow Americans."

About the Author

Howard Hill is a military veteran, retired correctional officer, and a former background actor in movies and television, as well as a lifetime weightlifter. He is an American historian with love a of God, country, and family. Also, he is a father of four great children and ten wonderful grandkids, as well as one great-grandchild.

May God bless our nation and our people and government.

www.ingramcontent.com/pod-product-compliance
Lightning Source LLC
Chambersburg PA
CBHW051418250726
48655CB00003B/1113